THE TRUMP BOOK OF INSULTS

T0115756

A POST HILL PRESS BOOK

The Trump Book of Insults:
An Adult Coloring Book
© 2016 by M. G. Anthony
All Rights Reserved

No part of this book may be reproduced, stored in a retrieval system, or transmitted by any means without the written permission of the author and publisher.

ISBN: 978-1-68261-226-2

Cover elements provided by vecteezy.com

Post Hill
PRESS

Post Hill Press
posthillpress.com

Printed in the United States of America

Major lightweight
with no credibility
(On Politico Reporter Ben Schreckinger)

flunkie
(On CNN Contributor Ana Navarro)

Nasty guy with
no heart
(On Evangelical Leader Russell Moore)

low life
(On Former Mayor of Philadelphia Michael Nutter)

MENTAL
BASKETCASE
(ON TALK SHOW HOST GLENN BECK)

Unbelievably nasty,
mean enabler
(On Hillary Clinton)

Spoiled brat without a properly functioning brain
[On Senator Rand Paul]

REALLY DUMB
PUPPET
(OR COLUMNIST MARC THIESSEN)

Couldn't be elected
dog catcher
(On Former New York Governor George Pataki)

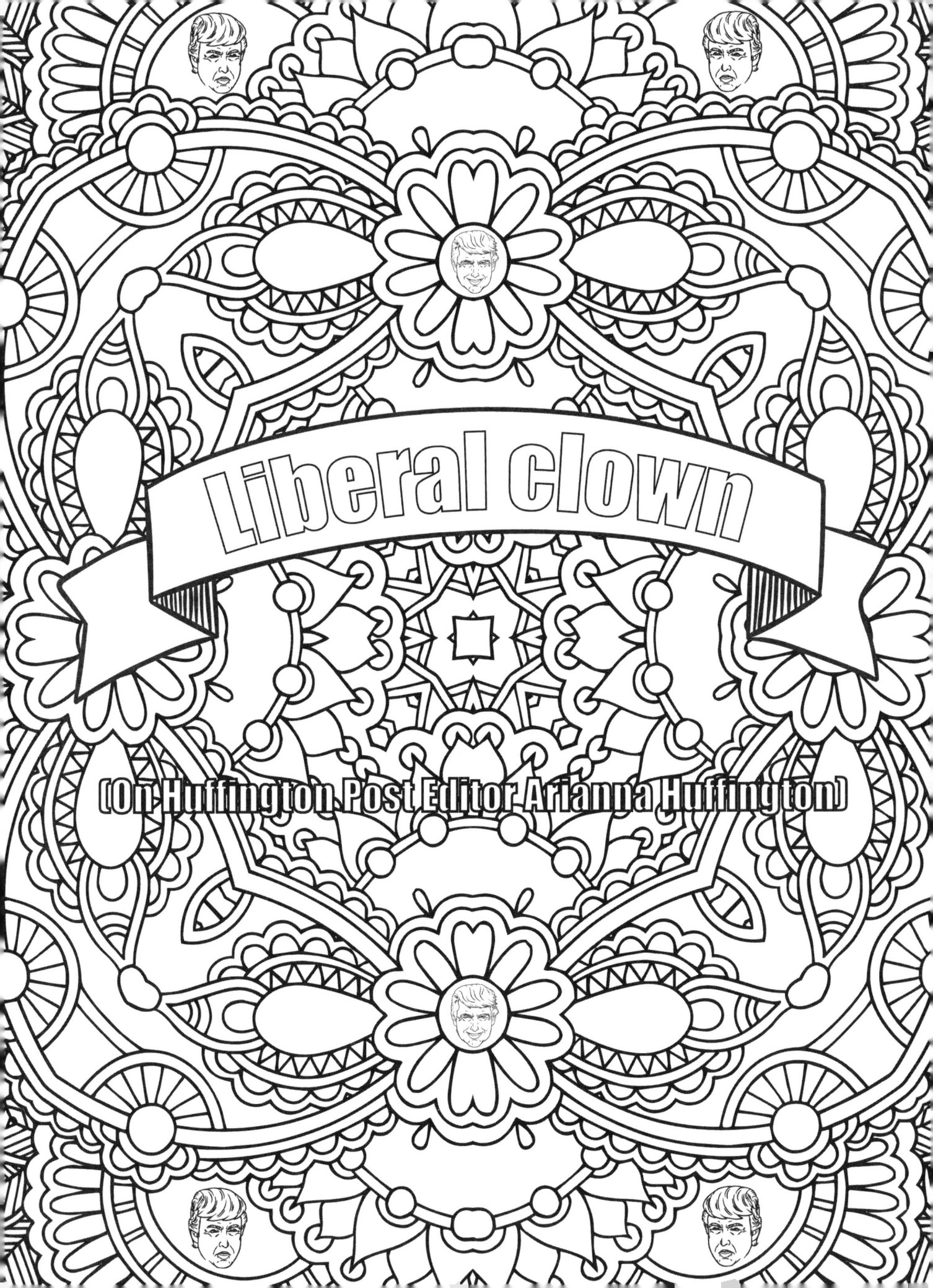
Liberal clown
(On Huffington Post Editor Arianna Huffington)

BORING, RAMBLING
AND
NON-SUBSTANTIVE
(ON PRESIDENT BARACK OBAMA'S
STATE OF THE UNION ADDRESS)

Wants to look cool, but it's far too late
(On Former Presidential Candidate Jeb Bush)

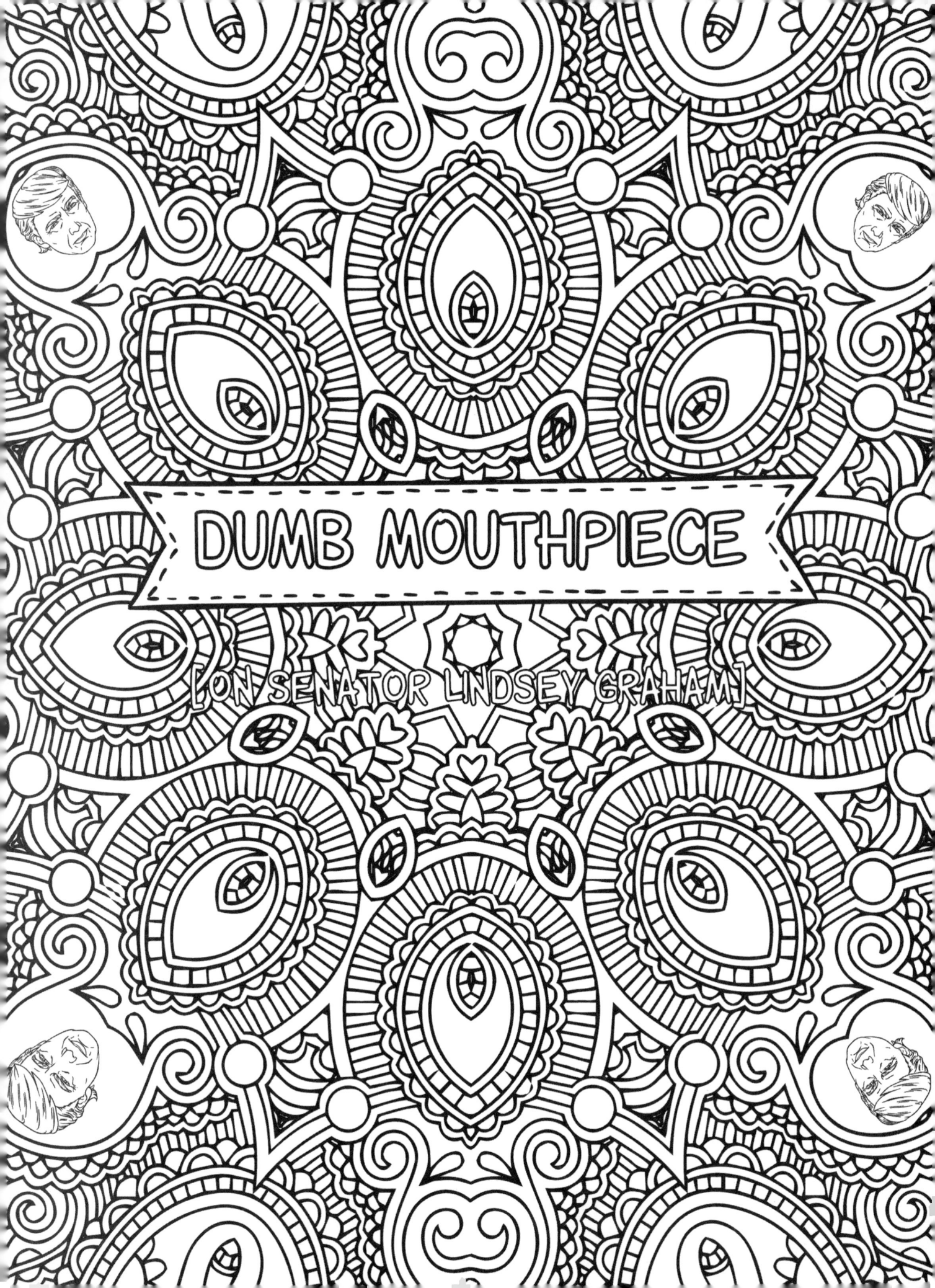
DUMB MOUTHPIECE
[ON SENATOR LINDSEY GRAHAM]

Total dud
(On Ohio Governor John Kasich)

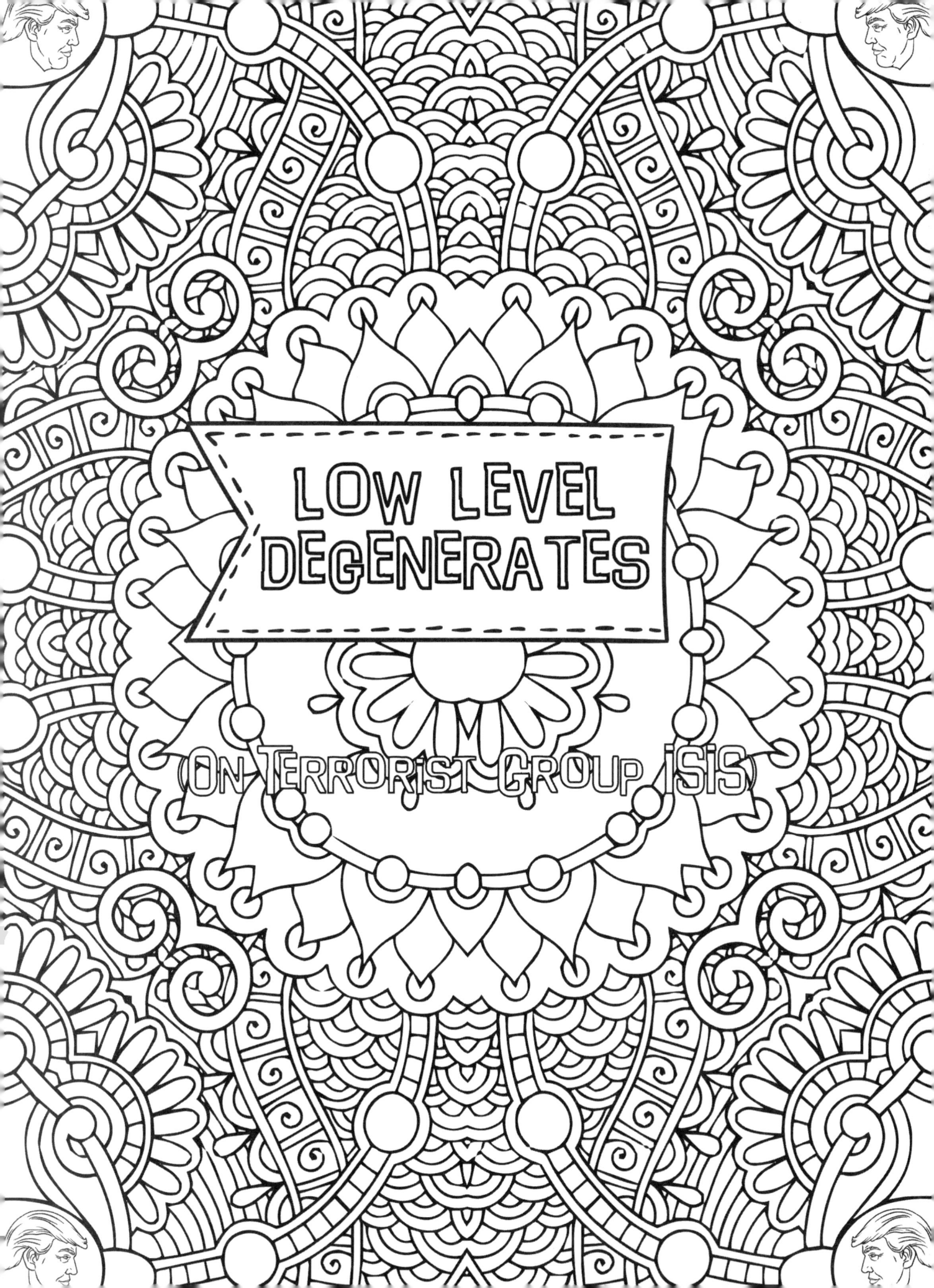
LOW LEVEL
DEGENERATES
(ON TERRORIST GROUP ISIS)

Always seems to be crying
(On Talk Show Host Glenn Beck)

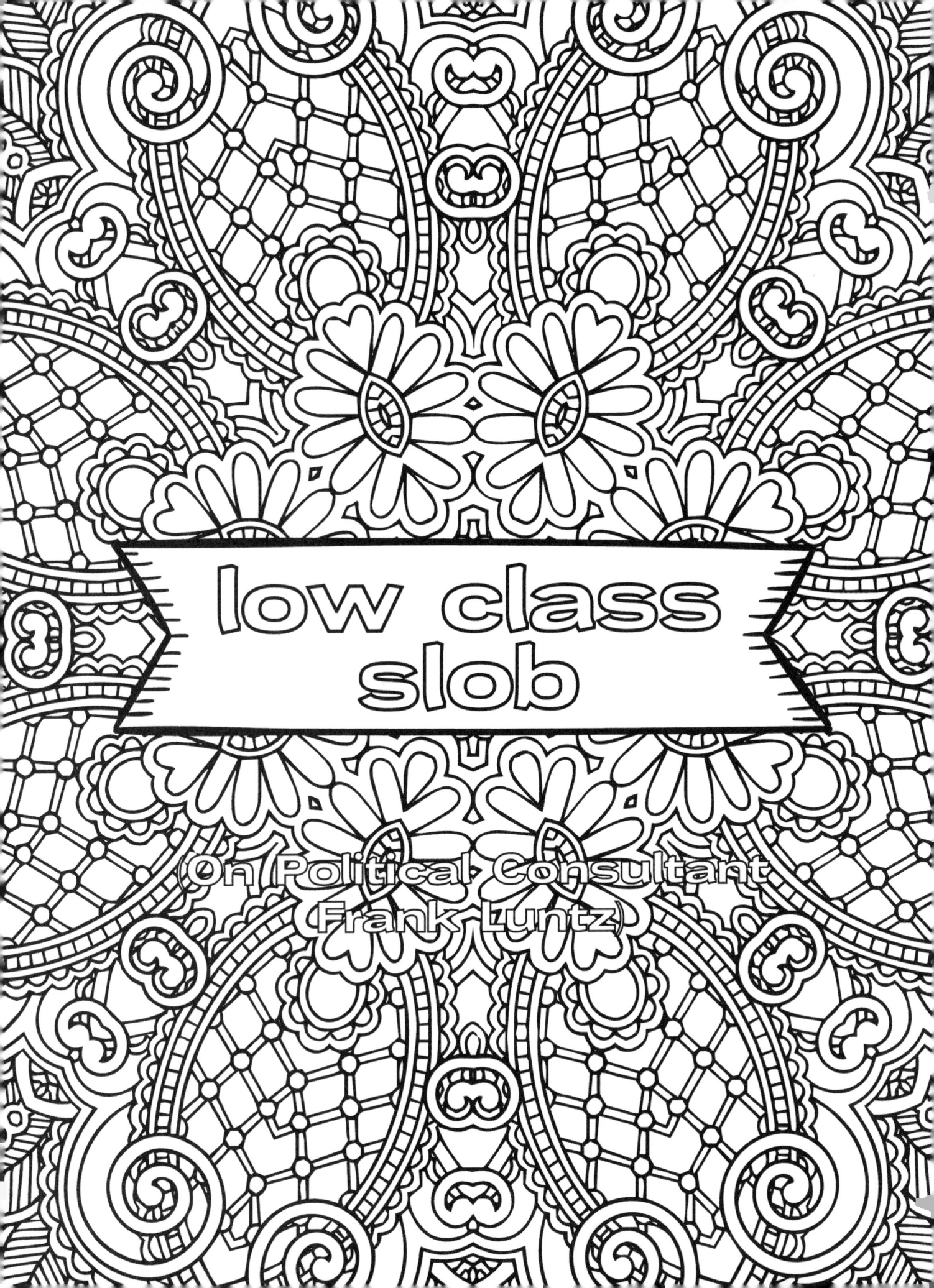
low class
slob
(On Political Consultant
Frank Luntz)

Hypocrite
(On Miss Universe 2014 Paulina Vega)

MAJOR SLEAZE
AND BUFFOON
(ON CONSERVATIVE COMMENTATOR
ERICK ERICKSON)

One of the dumbest political pundits on television
(On Fox News Contributor Chris Stirewalt)

Dummy
(On Former New Hampshire Governor John Sununu)

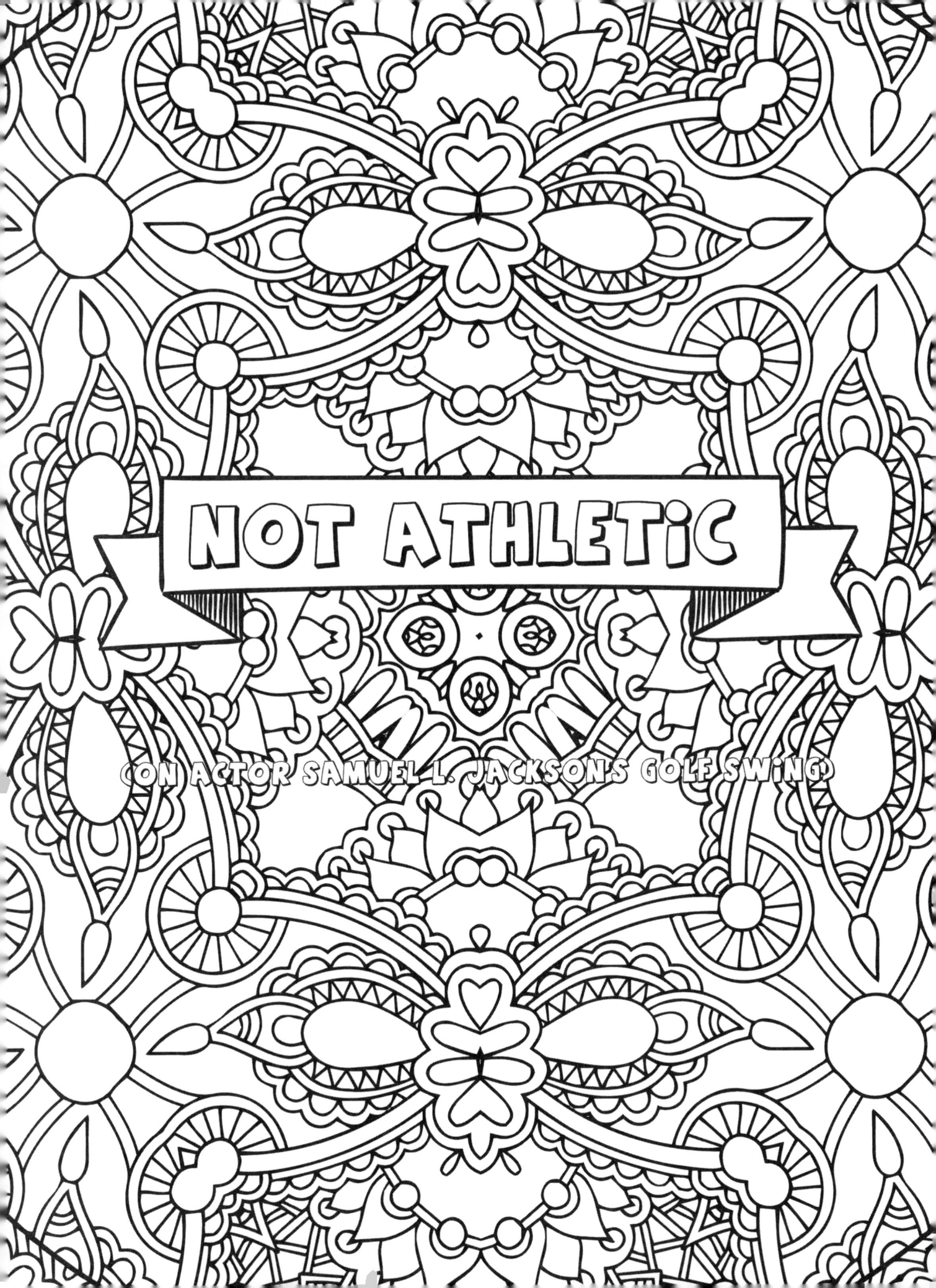
NOT ATHLETIC
(ON ACTOR SAMUEL L. JACKSON'S GOLF SWING)

Weak & ineffective
(On President Barack Obama)

Moron
(On Former Deputy White House
Chief Of Staff Karl Rove)

A PENCHANT FOR SEXISM
(ON FORMER PRESIDENT BILL CLINTON)

RATINGS STARVED
(On Television Show Meet The Press)

looks more like a
gym rat than a
U.S. Senator
(On United States Senator Ben Sasse)

A dumb guy who fails @
virtually everything
he touches
(On Political Consultant Stuart Stevens)

FIRED LIKE A DOG!
(ON POLITICAL ANALYST DAVID GREGORY)

Will NEVER Make America
Great Again
(On Former Presidential Candidate Jeb Bush)

Also available from

M.G. ANTHONY

Bestseller!

THE TRUMP COLORING BOOK
ISBN: 9781682610282
PRICE: $11.99

THE YOGA POSES ADULT COLORING BOOK
ISBN: 9781682611302
PRICE: $11.99

MEN IN UNIFORM ADULT COLORING BOOK
ISBN: 9781682611319
PRICE: $7.99

HAMILTON: AN ADULT COLORING BOOK
ISBN: 9781682612255
PRICE: $10.99

THE COLORING BOOK OF JEWISH SYMBOLS
ISBN: 9781682611913
PRICE: $9.99

Available Wherever Books Are Sold